"With a title playing off a phrase originating in William Tyndale's English translation of the New Testament, 'the quick and the dead,' Walter Bargen's *Too Quick for the Living* presents a livingness that is purely present, real, and realizable as walking the streets of Anytown, USA. From 'a lipsticked shot glass' to listening to Neil Young, from the Raptor Rehabilitation Center to the Leavenworth National Military Cemetery, we face, with these poems, the fragility and importance of connections, to the land and to each other. *Too Quick for the Living* resonates with the desire to pin things down, be it weather or grocery receipts, but it complicates itself with the wisdom of long experience, where any day, any event or relationship one tries to pin down comes back 'as fiction like all the rest.' It's an authentic and memorable journey."

—John Gallaher, author of *In a Landscape*

"If there is no god or fixed human nature, if life is so vulnerable to the sickle of death, then what is the nature of being, of mortality? And what are the limits of language or artistic rendering—expressed by Frank Zappa before the summer of love or found in a flea market photo in Kansas or a painting of the nineteenth-century financial district in London—and what must the poet bear? In *Too Quick for the Living*, Walter Bargen invites us to consider these questions as a descriptive act of consciousness in which the poet's existence becomes authenticated by 'living / through the failure to stop anything.' Stepping his Whitmanesque sentence shapes down the page in triadic lines, Bargen avoids the psychic inflation attendant of an artistic response to so serious a subject as the individual's confrontation with temporality. 'Sixty-five years / later,' he writes, 'I hear the insects in their August arias sharper / than ever, time sliced thinner and even more still.'"

—Marcus Cafagña, author of *The Broken World* and *Roman Fever*

Too Quick
for the Living

WALTER BARGEN

MOON CITY PRESS

This book is dedicated to Big Girl, Birthday, Sonny Boy, Squirrel, Nonee, Motor Mouse, Squee, Tortellini, Monk, Muffin Man, Mome, Sis, Bitey, Cuddles, Yelpy, Toot, Kit-Kat, Nutty, Mogely, Shorty, Shavey, Socks, Bobette, Tina, Mouser, June Bug, Snow Suit, Boney, Cowboy, and their decades of dedicated companionship. It is also dedicated to my daughter and son, Kale and Cedar.

In addition, a very large thank you goes to Mike Sleadd for our twelve-plus years of collaboration, including his patient work on the initial formatting of the manuscript for *Too Quick for the Living*.

And a heartfelt thank-you to Tom Dillingham and Matt Dube for reading early versions of this manuscript.

MOON CITY PRESS
Department of English
Missouri State University
901 South National Avenue
Springfield, Missouri 65897

First Edition
Copyright © 2017 by Walter Bargen
All rights reserved.
Published by Moon City Press, Springfield, Missouri, USA, in 2017.

Library of Congress Cataloging-in-Publication Data

Bargen, Walter
Too quick for the living: poems / Walter Bargen

2017956837

Further Library of Congress information is available upon request.

ISBN-10: 0-913785-97-0
ISBN-13: 978-0-913785-97-3

Cover and interior illustrated and designed by Charli Barnes

Edited by Lanette Cadle & Karen Craigo

Manufactured in the United States of America.

www.mooncitypress.com

ACKNOWLEDGEMENTS

My thanks to the editors of the following publications in which these
poems first appeared:

American Journal of Poetry, "Invasion of the Giant Tomatoes"
Big River Review, "The Bitterness of Forty Yards of Water"
Cavalier Magazine, "Family of Stars"
Concho River Review, "Dinner Party"
Cybersoleil, "Undocumented," "Miles"
Hawaii Pacific Review, "Nights with Oscar"
Heartland, "Pinko"
I-70 Review, "Gregorian End Times"
Laurel Review, "Kansas Freaks"
Moon City Review, "Day's Receipt," "Exposure," "Forced Busing," "State of
the Art"
Natural Bridge, "Absence of Elephants"
Ozark Mountain Review, "Photogenic"
Pinyon Poetry, "A History of Glass Not Found on a Hill in Tennessee,"
"Fewer of These"
Plume, "Utterly Again"
Poetry Pacific, "Redwood"
Vox Populi, "Circus Coil," "Gorilla God," "Vaudeville Visigoths," "Paint by
Numbers"

Anthologies:
"Kansas Freaks" appears in *Begin Again: 150 Kansas Poems*, Woolsey
Memorial Press (2012).

"Photogenic" and "Wounded God" appear in *Yonder Mountain: Ozark
Anthology*, University of Arkansas Press (2013).

"Seeds of Revolution (Potato Myths)" appears in *Spud Songs: An Anthology of
Potato Poems*, Helicon Nine Press (1999).

"Ashes (Fishy Business)" appears in the anthology *Urban Voices: 51 poems,
51 poets*, San Francisco Bay Press (2014).

"Ascending the Mountain Slowly" appears in *Pushing the Envelope*, Lamar University Press, 2015.

Avian Perspectives" appears in *Thinking Continental*, University of Nebraska Press, 2017.

Too Quick for the Living

4

Too Quick
for the Living

WALTER BARGEN

MOON CITY PRESS

In the middle of your life
You cast aside the brittle flame.
      —Brenda Hillman

It will be strange
Knowing at last it couldn't go on forever.
      —Mark Strand

Ascending the Mountain Slowly

The first line to your letter forgotten as I sit down to respond.
The phone rings. Someone needs
dried flowers for a vase in a room far away. Her life doesn't
yearn for green, or something
rooting through humus, groping around stones, shoving aside
all but water and light.

She wants what's left. Her room is all corners and walls.
It's hard for her to imagine more
than the frail and brittle. Dried cockscomb, stiff baby's breath.
Perhaps something exotic
and common as the dry hiss of rattlesnake grass
as she passes the table.
Whatever opens the room without opening the door.
Now I have forgotten the second and third lines of your letter.
I open the window beside the desk
and hear the relentless chirring of cicadas and their hard-
bodied backup.
It's the choking of an engine in another season, their spring-loaded legs
and unsteady wings
clicking and rasping. In the middle of the field, the oak a dying traffic jam.

More of your carefully crafted lines have died in the scalpeled
schedule of silences.
Before I address what's left, as if I might suture sentences back together,
I notice the envelope
is imprinted with a picture of a crumpled envelope.
Faux fractal refuse removed from

a wastebasket and smoothed for use again, as if for a love
that's always running
toward an abrupt end. It's worse than my last thought.
Only your signature is still
visible below gray clouds. What was it you were telling me?

That only four hibiscus clay trees
are still alive on the slopes of the Nounou Mountains?
That the last p'ouli
spent four years in a cage deep in tropical forest singing
for a mate that never
came then died of West Nile Virus? I fold my letter
to be postmarked years ago.

The Bitterness of Forty Yards of Water

The song of the turtle dove mourning is the song
Of the turtle dove wooing.

—Yehuda Amichai

A place flooded out of existence
more than once: two thirtyish guys, two six-packs, one car parked
on the bank, one letter to be written

to one beautiful woman
who has moved downriver to St. Louis, or up the Mississippi to
Minneapolis, they're uncertain

of everything but the move
and the necessity of writing a letter that I read two decades later.
They report the weather—

early summer cold front
cleared away the heat. From the throne of a black '64 Ford Galaxy,
they attend to their too-quiet

kingdom and fret,
unacknowledged legislators of the world, more unacknowledged
than ever. The muddy maudlin current

wobbling with the second beer.
It's still the first page as the river rears toward *the endless,*
the deep vast, stupid ocean.

What is the sound of four hands
writing one letter—the finny language of fish? What to call
themselves, species they will never know.

Truth larger than truth
there on the sun-bleached white paper. She is lost swimming
        far out in time: concert harpist, jazz pianist,

playing her father's 78s
in the basement before it flooded. Billy Preston drifts in from
        the radio of a nearby parked car.

They're anchored to the music
of this bend in the river, the opening snap of the fourth beer,
        they're secure in becoming part of her past.

They report emptiness
on Walnut Street: There is always bitterness in any endeavor of love.
        Across forty yards of water,

two young women
sun themselves on a wing dike, smoke, drink beer, leave before any
        overtures. Swallows skim the roiling surface,

threading dusk and insects
together. River and simmering light, a lipsticked shot glass
        set on night's edge.

for Frank & Paul

More Moses Than Neil Young

> *Down by the river ...*
> —Neil Young

Maybe the year was 1968,
            maybe '69, always the indefinite
boundaries of visions we were working,

Down by the river:
            hitting hard on *down,*
       missing the turn,
careening into an embankment,
            holding on to *by,*
delaying the separation of body a moment longer,
            a quick falling jab at *the*
as if still panting through the windshield,
            then *riv-er,*
two flooded syllables headed down,
            embracing the first as if you might not let go
of the steering wheel,
            then the slow, just-in-time breaking
of the second—
            four decades, this song flowing
from vinyl to CD to streaming,
            from life to life.

☾

And that's the beauty of it,
            sitting here on the first official day
of autumn, warmth
            more than we'd like,
more than enough,
         the breeze a fevered amniotic wash

as we huddle in the shadows
                                of the womblike riverbank cottonwood
palisade, listening to a friend's story:

            A baby floats past
                                face down in the river,
            she shouts and leaps into the johnboat
                                starting the cantankerous motor
            with the first try.
                                The baby from a camp upstream,
            in the water maybe five minutes,
                                survives, and the retired,
            childless school teacher has her first rebirth.

That's the beauty of it,
                                the braiding currents
at each sweeping meander, sandy syllables
                                sighing south past where we sit,
nothing to do but listen and watch five egrets,
                                their white feathers
mounting the wing dike's
                                murky backwater swirls,
and all afternoon we dryly abandon
                                ourselves "Down by the River."

UNDOCUMENTED

What if there is no stoplight, nowhere to where,
     no turn to make?
Missed in a blink of an eye. Adobe rearview dust.
     Universe expanding and unrelenting.
A name written on every boarded-up house.
     Forward, foreword, foreclosed.
Sidewalk and alley alike. No difference walking up and down,
     back and forth. Fifteen minutes
of fame emblazoned on bathroom stalls. Offers grandiose.
     Phone numbers algorithms.
Desire demands recall. Stars beyond stars.
     That's all anyone came for,
to pass through, not to know an end. Not sure how
     to get back, only more boned exposure.

Kicked up dust—such theatrics—all these overweight
     stick-figure saguaros
caught in centuries-long bank-holdup poses. Chased by
     unrelenting posses of light.
So laughable: All they walk away with is a pocketful of stones.
     Leaving the arroyo
sure that they've thrown these stones before,
     hot as a rain of asteroids.
It's what hits the rabbit behind a floppy ear
     that kills.
The man from the other side of the duplex universe says all
     he wanted was to caress pulsing fur.
There's an arc to nonsense, sorrow always in the missing.
     It's the straight line off the map that kills us.

MILES

A roadside biblical plague:
fifteen-foot-long steel grasshopper painted yellow, a relative
of Jiminy Cricket without his toe-tapping fiddle, and his companion,
close in length,
a sheet-metal-scaled crocodile with a grin quick to disarm
any victim who might stop to take a photograph of these two
sitting beside repaired tractors, trailers, balers, wide-wheeled herbicide sprayers.

Outside town on the way to the next town,
in the middle of a field surrounded by scrub oaks, upright
and wedding white,
though the seams are showing from years of reeling sunlight,
a drive-in theater screen. A hundred feet away
the projection booth, concession stand, windows broken out
and the growing crowd,
basketball-tall sunflowers, their yellow-petaled, seed-heavy faces
turned toward the weathering screen,
straining to read the too-fast scrolling credits
of sun.

In the river bottoms, the fields are tabletop flat
with an imperceptible tilt toward the Gulf. A billboard warns
of the world's largest pecan.
Two miles ahead, gawkers slow down to observe or do battle.
Along one edge of a parking lot,
a bulbous, mottled concrete monster, fossilized blimp,
that each year sinks deeper into the pine-pitted sandy loam,
as pounds, pecks,
bushels are hoisted into trunks and trucks.

The barn, board and batten darkened
to the color of days-old coffee, stands as sentinel and guide
to the mile-long furrows
that end inches from its drooping vine-strangled walls.
It calls together the fall congregations of corn and soybeans,
its corrugated tin roof intact, rusted deep as dried blood
after another midweek bar fight.
Lettering visible from any crop-dusting plane
or from a mile up the road, its fifty-year-old advertisement
for Coca-Cola drinks in
the silver-scripted cocaine-flashes of sun.

Gray scar of road,
and beyond the ditch conversations arc between telephone poles,
where wind's moan unravels, undiminished at the horizon
with everything still left to say.
No matter how many times it's repeated, pressed, impressed,
repetition is the only truth.
Heaven remains out there with all the empty miles.

for Bill Wells

Wounded God

Dismal laundry, a hunter's mishap, a dusky-feathered hanging heap,
oversight or under—
a miscalculation of flight. A wind-driven day, light ironed flat
across fields,
bristling sedge underscoring the burnished closeting
of evening. A wide feathered face
turns slowly, hooked yellow beak half open—tired, defenseless.

Coonhound that follows its nose as the one and only direction,
she has inhaled
acres of field and found under the last thin scars of snow
the bodies of a frozen mouse,
a vole, all pulled from her eager mouth. Restrained, we turn toward
the house, jog the half-mile back
to find a large cardboard box and leather gloves.

At the gate, caught between sun's afterglow and the uprising
half-moon, I can't see to untangle the owl.
In headlights, I cut on either side of its twisted wing.
It stares suspended in its own failed flight. Talons pried
from the wire, I see
that its left-wing feathers are shredded from flying nowhere.
Placed in the box, the bird still as road kill.
I'm possessed, hoping to undo this evening, not remembering
my many flights into the undone.

At the Raptor Rehabilitation Center, I sign a form giving the owl
into their care. In the hallway,
the attendant's thick gloves lift the body and find the bird's eyes
wide open.
It shakes itself awake, stands with a sense
of unabashed decorum, as if this happens every day, one wing
folded elegantly,
the other straight as a ragged broom

that's swept too many miles of wind. Brown tufted ears, feathers the colors
of fall fields, quarter-sized pupils,
hand-sized talons, it stands with a wounded, defiant elegance.

Strand of barbed wire still embedded in its shoulder joint.
The attendant holds out little chance for recovery.
I propose the wing be amputated and the bird be kept
for exhibition. I'm told it's illegal
to amputate a wing beyond the first joint. It's illegal for me to keep the bird
and it's illegal for them to keep the bird alive.
I plead beauty, but there are no guarantees this night.

When death calls we pretend not to hear, refuse to listen as long
as we can. There is no one to blame.
Not even our petty selves when finally we hear too clearly.
I think of my son as I drive home.
He's passing through Amarillo, past seven high-finned Cadillacs
half-buried and forever driving
deeper into panhandle dust. He'll continue through the dark,
wind down through
Sandia Pass, where brakes fail and cars are swallowed
by out-of-control semis, where lights of benighted
Albuquerque spread over the desert
as he heads on to Phoenix, hoping he will be the bird that rises
out of the ashen sweep of stars.

Photogenic

We stop for gas. I knock my sunglasses off the seat, pick them up off
the asphalt before a darker vision runs them down.
Cameraless, we lament, wish we had brought one: the cheap never-used,
antiquated, 35-millimeter in the sock drawer
or the digital in the back of a closet. We begin to share pictures—

click—flock of fifteen wild turkeys strutting over a greening
hillside pasture—
click—loose line of white cows working their way around a cattail-
choked pond toward a weathered barn—
click—condom nailed to a tree beside the river where we lunch—

click—cable-suspended canoe twenty feet above the ground between
two oaks, its two black plywood
silhouettes, seated straight through the year, their wooden legs cramping,
they paddle as a gust of wind almost capsizes them
into currents of humid air—

click—owl or hawk that we pass too quickly to know, one wing
angled upright out of the pavement—
click—through a town named Plato, far from any city-state, no Socrates,
no Aristotle,
no exiled poets, more likely white chickens by a red wheelbarrow.

EXPOSURE

The flea-market photo
bought fifty miles south of here, printed on stiff gray cardstock,

with the town's name in silver
across the bottom. Maybe there's a relative who still lives there.

The man pictured stern,
severe, dour, nearly a morgue shot. But even in black and white,

nothing stops his gray steel stare penetrating the camera
and the other end of a century. Behind the foot-long beard

tapering to a blunt point, the face
of old-time religion, ready to suffer, ready to make others suffer.

At work, my ex-Peace Corps
coworker exclaims, Oh no, it's the camera.

In Niger, the people were
so animated: laughing, singing, ready to play, but when he aimed

his camera, all activity stopped.
Everyone buttoned their shirts, buttoned down their collars,

straightened their dresses, grimly lined up
to be executed for posterity. He stands up behind his desk,

both arms nailed to the sides
of his pine-board-straight body, shoulders squared,

chin thrust slightly up,
his face cold clay, as if he'd been in the office all day.

for Robin Albee

KANSAS FREAKS

Once in a while a touch like the above.

—Joseph Cornell

If I have to remember something about 1966, let it be Frank Zappa
and the Mothers of Invention,
their first vinyl record, *Freak Out.* It was Christmas vacation
and, looking for something to set me apart
from the dull Midwest, I bought the album for its psychedelic neon cover
before I'd heard the word psychedelic.
My favorite line, sung longingly, "With hair growing out every hole
in me," as if their one wild moment
had already fallen to the barbershop floor. Perhaps they were right, thirty
years later, the band broken up,
Frank dead of prostate cancer, my turntable up in a puff
of smoke, signaling
the century's end, and no more listening to scratchy vinyl.

In *Help, I'm a Rock*, Frank always a little grandiose
and self mocking, snubbed
the sentimental Simon & Garfunkel song *I Am a Rock.*
In falsetto he sings,
It can't happen here. Of course it could, and it was,
and if it wasn't,
where then might it happen, in every hair follicle in Kansas,
teasing me to join in
as I lay on the floor between hi-fi speakers.

Thirty years later, at a luncheon held in juvenile detention, I'm losing interest,
it's not happening here.
I unfold a newspaper laid on a chair, read that the state of Kansas, defined
by geography not song,
reviewed all bronze roadside historical plaques. State officials decided
to remove
the story of "The Bloody Benders," not because on the high prairie

a mile northwest of the Mounds
and thirteen miles from the town of Parsons where the Bender family
built a one-room house
in 1871, where travelers who sat for a meal
were bludgeoned, robbed,
and shoved through a trap door in the floor—eleven bodies,
skulls crushed, unearthed in 1873.

It's not the horrific, not the festering frontier, but Kate,
the Bender daughter,
the self-proclaimed healer and spiritualist, who contacted
dead relatives for the locals,
who lured men *with a tigerish grace*, this *voluptuous girl*
is officially offensive.
Death can only be flat and lonely as Kansas. This life of heat,
humidity, wheat, the official one.
The dead left to God, mass murder to a bronzed plaque.
And Frank sings on remastered CDs,
Kansas, Kansas, it can't happen here.

AVIAN PERSPECTIVES

Waking in a strange bed, I'd forgotten magpies

                                until this morning.
Beyond the window, one flies over the weathered picket fence,

                                black-white
staccato wing beat: moonlit cloud against night sky,
snow-streak shadowed mountain,

                                manic-depressive,
winged declaration of union-disunion.
The long-tailed bird perches

                                in a bare cottonwood,
on the far side of the creek.

☾

Cold sentinels along Kansas dirt roads,

                                stone fence posts
subdivide the vast curve of horizon.

                                Nothing
like the Pacific's stoic statues

                  facing centuries of hypnotic waves,

                                their heavy volcanic
brows softening to blank stares,

                      having seen it all, all over again.
From corner post
to corner post at the shores of salty prairie

                              tall grasses surf wind.

☾

Immigrant claims of ancestors:

                              a stretched, four-starred
steel rusting toward the future, stone posts
                              grooved by wire
that wind never tires tuning

                              to an infinite low moan,
a tireless sea-voice to an ear sinking in dust.

                    ☾

The unpolished granite

                              at the limits of homesteads,
far fields, dry gulches, smoky hills,
                              a foundation of grassy outlines,
clumps of jonquils, and rotting wheel spokes.
                              Rectangular, upright,
chest-high squared limestone slabs,
                              and these high plains
scarred by a single tree and magpie
                              slowly flying over dry seas.

                              for Tom Carlough

House Lessons

In the newspaper's real estate want ads,
the over-eager smile and architecturally coiffed hair invite trust, confidence,
honesty, a graciousness as you are laid down comfortably numb
into a lifetime of debt.

☾

A tutor house priced to sell.
Chance to live a life's lessons within four walls. Teacher with a solid foundation.
No cracked,
shifting circumstances. Sump pump new, prepared for unexpected floods
of errant learning.
Arched doorways no longer just for the kingly. Queenly centuries
of thick-walled pasts reduced to Sheetrock
and layers of wallpaper crossed by wandering wainscoting.
Termite inspected,
home loan ready. Lovely neighborhood lined with crowning oaks.

☾

How many houses
have come to inhabit me? A couple of years, late sixties, Ross Street,
storing friends' motorcycles who'd decided
to travel more lightly, quietly, unsure of a destination other than sunrise
in empty fields outside Oakley, Kansas,
halfway between nowheres, but a little farther west a certainty;
then to be awakened too early by the backup clang,
the clatter of garbage trucks in downtown Denver, the smoky pall
of the living already dulling the day.

☾

Between rooms, between houses,
baptized in volcanic-hot springs in the snow-peaked
Jemez Mountains,
mesmerized in a deep gash across the Taos Plateau,
the Rio Grande Gorge,
back against a spiral petroglyph, the amniotic warmth
ringed by blackened basalt boulders,
the snowmelt a cold glass, where the steep canyon walls ripped a ribbon
of stars out of the sky.

☾

Bells of Pacific waves ring, friends found and lost
the same day: on the other side of dunes,
around a bend in the trail, turn in the road, end of the street, breathing in
the thin air of the Sierras,
breathing in the scorched Mojave, the smog-cough of L.A.,
sleeping in dust
of abandoned Venice buildings, night punctuated by ocean cries,
standing beside rundown
beach houses waiting for mercy, waiting for other houses.

☾

Parked in a row
in the Ross Street house basement garage on another hot rented night,
admiring the chrome,
the thick grip of the curved-back handle bars, the throaty motor
of a 750cc Norton, the sudden urge to pray
on the stars, to breathe in what has yet to happen, I shoot up
the cracked drive

onto the dark pavement, overpowered, out of control, racing up
the wooden steps across the street,

stopping, stunned, dethroned on the porch of yet another house.

2

One of many paintings that hung
in the living room of her apartment:
a broad nineteenth century London financial-district
      street, nearly abandoned or just empty
            except for the soul of moonlight muted
by backlit broken clouds, and a cloaked
            rider leaning forward, the horse
galloping against the stillness.
A viewer can hear hooves echoing off
      the coal-stained Romanesque buildings.
            It's easy to imagine hiding behind one
of the shadowy fluted marble columns,
            hoping not to be found out, handed
      the urgent message, that always
arrives too late for fate, for destiny,
      for the tired rider.

I set the gilded frame outside one overcast
                  spring day, rain a threat.
      The painting upright, backed by books,
at a slight angle to the vertical, facing away
            from the darkly muted sun that could
                  almost be moonlight. An odd
centerpiece for a wrought-iron picnic table.
            I take ten photographs.
      The developing done, the appraisal requested,
the photographs mailed to Christie's.
      Odd, no matter how I tried
            to avoid the flash's glare, each frame held
a bright blind eye, as if the oil embraced
            this dull perspective. Her husband, recently dead,
      this was her inheritance, a European painting
hanging on a forgotten Midwestern wall.
      Informed it was not an original, not worth

the hundred thousand dreamed dollars—
just a copy by a student studying the master's
   strokes, the tradition of the time. Worth
  something, but not enough for the remains of
a lifetime.

       ☾

What about the Sumerian pottery handles
    used for bookends, the cuneiform clay tablets that
  sat on a shelf with their message
of bushels received and promised, the noseless bust
  of a pharaoh mounted on a small steel post,
    the brass wheel of fire encircling the many-
armed Kali, dancing by herself on the howling
    upturned gutted body of creation, her necklace
  of skulls writhing in lamplight?
In what century are they again lost or stolen?

In a penny jar shoved to the backsplash
    beside the kitchen sink,
  the head of Lincoln acrobatically stacked
on the tarnished head of Lincoln,
  and there a small glint, a drop of silver
    toward the bottom of a copper circus.
Pennies heaped on the table, I hold
    a small thick coin, an imperfect circle,
  edges broadly rounded. The portrait
ancient, a heroic Greek profile
  with unkempt swirls of hair, the lion's head
    hood swallowing the back
of his head as if he were being devoured
    by the power of history. The reverse,
  a god seated, staff in hand, eagle
at his feet. Later, we would know it's

a hemidrahm, one Alexander the Great
might have spent in his empire. Later still,
  it was a present, the small change of our past
    that fills jars and gets casually spent.

☾

Who can say what happened? What's left,
      ashes. Friends wondering. Eight years
  ago, she turned away. Refused to answer
phone calls, knocks on the door, shouts
    through open windows, letters, except
        for the occasional encounters in grocery stores,
enough to say fine and return quickly to her midnight list.
      She must have found aisles
    that no one wandered looking for cheese
and cereal. What's left is a 9-1-1 call,
    an unidentified voice, dirty pots and pans
        scattered across the living room floor,
dozens of jeans worn once, panties bedded
        in each one, the pockets stuffed with dirty
      tissue, nothing her size, her car in storage
but no record of its location,
    no records of bank transactions
        or utility bills, her monthly rent always paid
with money orders. Years ago she turned to art.

for Betty Thompson

Measure

I didn't know sadness could go on for so long
could go all the way back to lying beside
an open bedroom window where the world
outside was cut sharp and clean by light.

Inside, deep in shadows, still and alone,
a breeze, something begged for
or borrowed from another lifetime
beyond this one sun-blistered mid-afternoon,

sifted by the metal window screen.
There listening to the rise and fall of the cicada
chorus, the steady rasp of a small thing
sharpening light and time to cut deeper.

Lying there, arms and legs splayed to be cool,
too young to know of Da Vinci's man drawn
in a circle, that I was a horizontal replica
on a rectangular mattress, and now left wondering

was that naked, frizzy-haired man part of the encircling,
the center, or trapped in his own measure? Sixty-five years later,
I hear insects in their August arias sharper
than ever, time sliced thinner and ever more still.

Nights with Oscar

Diesel exhaust chokes the room. Engines work overtime.
Naked body pounds
against naked body. In perdition's factory,
they push poverty's gravity
another thirty days
and balance their lives with time-and–a-half,
the monthly paycheck a week's resurrection.
Dark fumes, not just the windows open to the street,
but the oily rags of love ready to combust.

Nothing so vague and distant as the last-minute struggle to get
beyond or back—
the distinct longing for both. Names no longer familiar,
the granite syllables turn unstable
and a wet month changes everything to lichen and shadow.
Take the slippery step backwards,
no stunt man to take the fall. No one able to reconstruct
the complexity of a single big-tent dying dive,
not even a second's decomposing. If not dead already,
hands folded
over chest, the light too quick for the living.

Across the floor and up the flaming walls, eyes tired beyond belief,
sweat allegiance
to the reddened, rubbed-raw, capillaried visions of days to come.
Blues the backstop
to searing speed, to this backstroking absence, fingers interlocked
in prayer to what
is happening and what hasn't in every direction.

Even then no one can be certain:
who is still standing in the center ring, who's crumpled on the curb,
who's lying in the alley,
who's hanging from the rusty fire escape, kicking their legs
in the air, who's saving the burning clowns.

A History of Glass Not Found on a Hill in Tennessee

The bottle, the thick green-glass kind, the wavy cool aquarium kind, recently washed up

in a ditch, half buried in leaves, half full of something that momentarily defies gravity before sloshing out. Forty years old, nothing precise except in intent, not a languorous iced drink on a café patio in the shade of an umbrella, where a broad valley with a train too far away to hear as it winds its way along a river to the blue sweep of the Mediterranean that opens just beyond the round table where friends quench their thirst for friends on a Sunday in 1939, the final year that wide-brimmed hats of strollers could be gaily white and not the smoke of amnesia, the gesture of a world gone numb and blind with terror.

Lying on its side by the door, recalling an artifact of revolution, the green-tinted glass

tainted with reddish streaks of benzene, became something solid to hurl, the saturated cloth wick a candle tracing the dimming hallways of history, an ashen explanation even as the flames radiated, but even this incendiary moment is incomplete, so not this bottle, either, but the one beached by the door, filled with pieces of glass found too late and never enough to make a whole, the scalpel-sharp edges smoothed in the incessant lathe of waves, dull as the featureless sky that dissolves into horizon, the horizon always more distant, announcing the evening's tidal vespers as the barefoot changeling walks ceaselessly by the edgeless water and sand, stooping to collect the worthless glitter of beach glass, the many bottles now in a single one, much as we find on mantles and desks, the models of three-masted ships, sunk on centuries' dusty shoals, the wreckage of destinations and departures, safely miniaturized, and in a dusty corner there's one bottle with a lighthouse inside, its light forever flashing a warning.

The child fills the jar with water, holds it up to the sun, proud and dazzled by this broken collection of breaking light, her bronzed skin a beacon to her parents who are themselves dissolving into shards, much as the wineglass, round base rising into the stem that balances the tulip-shaped emptiness that opens to their mouths, ferments their speech, sweet and dry, and then placed into a paper bag, is laid on its side, waiting for the right moment to seal a vow—crushed under foot, splintered, the hoped-for shards to prick more years than can be counted, and yet the bottle upright beside the door fills with rain water and mosquito larvae as it waits to be recycled.

Absence of Elephants

The window is not an eye
even when it blinks with sunset, lamplight, car beams
sweeping across the driveway.

The window is a mouth.
Wide open this last night of November, gulping down wind
until the room is fully cold.

The stoic cat shivers
under the desk. Beyond the porch light's ringed reach,
the world collapses.

Something moves through
the thousand brittle leaves. The studied step
of the threatening or the threatened.

Last night in bed,
the house was wrapped in a flamboyant scarf of flames.
A liquored, lacquered light

evaporated across
the roof's shingles. Nothing remains.
Everything remains.

Night's charcoal shadows
trumpet. Where is the heat to redream a house?
The house a realtor's rustic:

plotted, trenched, wired,
consumed in a web of trees. Enough for a widow's
wait. Another day, the sun's

claret hour glass
about to empty. The house sways, lumbers
off toward the next extinction.

ASHES

Mid-afternoon, a hot dog vendor burrows into the shade
of an umbrella,
waiting for the next tide of traffic as the stoplight moons green.
A hickory-scented fog rises
from the handmade stack of a portable barbeque cut from
a rusting barrel abandoned in the parking lot.
The most obvious member of this street corner rises high
above the mustard and ketchup.
I drive encircling the circular fence in a country that likes
everything straight if not erect.
I take a photo, the world's tallest Corinthian column, 154 feet,
a relic hunting
for its temple. It towers over neglected, mostly abandoned
low-storied red-brick buildings.
A pressure-relief standpipe for an 1871 steam-driven water system.
Nearby the Carter Carburetor Corporation
with busted-out windows. Random white, green, slate-colored panes,
surround dark voids,
victims of wanton rock and gunshot. A voice closes in from
half a block back, shouting, *Wait,*
as he hurries the sidewalk, crosses the street. Quickly, I turn to
the car, lock the doors, close the driver's window,
start the engine, but don't pull away. Next to me, the man shouts, pulls up
his stained T-shirt revealing
a slightly bulging belly—a round hill stood on its side,
nearly barren but for a few blades
of curling black grass. He yells, *No gun,* and lets his shirt fall back
to his waist. He needs food
for two teenagers huddled in a doorway. His breath 70 proof.
I give him a handful
of quarters and dimes, as he stares at the ashes of coins
still in the tray.

The Usual Regrets

Even if it's just around the corner, and it's not,
with creeks to cross, one-way city streets to follow,
mind to set straight, it's always a long drive home.
At every stoplight, traffic backs up, the serpentine
snarl of brake lights constricting patience.

Across the intersection, the stop sign spits
rusting Pintos, Gremlins, Fiestas, one at a time.
From the entrance ramp, the highway tongues
miles of concrete as he slips from one
exhaust-slavered lane to another.

Hoping for a faster way, he tunes in to a classic
oldies station, sixties tunes, spinning them with claims
of the greatest rock 'n' roll decade. He ups
the volume as Blood, Sweat, and Tears
belts out, *You make me so very happy,*

and he can't remember the exact year,
maybe '67, but for the briefest moment,
he's headed in that direction, a forty-year-old wind
bellowing paisley shirts and bell bottoms
wide enough to hide a second girlfriend,

and the time a couple of Vietnam vets drunk
on defeat punched at his passing, a Quicksilver
concert just around the corner, and he believed it all,
and wants to believe it again. This road disappears
into its own distance and he can't catch up.

Through the windshield the sky opens, cirrus
clouds remix Daylight Savings Time. If he can slip
a seasonal hour here and there, why not decades?
Why not crave that crazed time again?
Why not make each other happy?

FORCED BUSING

This is what the old do after giving up the future—recalibration:
fifty the new forty, sixty the new fifty.
They fall back as they stumble forward, denial the viable strategy.
Holstered to their chests,
the concealed weapon of their heart fires blanks at every party, every
birthday that creeps closer
through the underbrush of days. No candles, no cards, not even a half-day
off from work,
certainly not a vacation to hide within or without. This is what the old do,
grow more
and more stateless as borders blur, and it's not just retinal detachment,
visions clouded
by storms of floaters, the cascade of cataracts turning traffic lights
into shimmering pools, macular degeneration
abandoning the tunneled light for a dark room in eternity. The old buy
buses to convert
into destinations but are quickly lost in installing the lightweight cabinets
with fixed shelves
to slow the breakage, lost in the bolting of mattress frame to floor and wall
to lessen
the careening, and too soon confused come to believe there is time
to sleep off another chance,
to awaken from all the comas of loves' past collisions. The old
bleach the water reservoir,
secure the propane tank, reread the instructions for the composting toilet,
grow tired of the inventions,
the ingenuity, the space savers, the estate planning, the automatic
bill payments, and resort
to realphabetizing the map drawer, choosing another direction,
this one too much
like the last one, segregating distance from the distant.

for Sam Stowers

REDWOOD

This spring afternoon two shovels
booted into the soft ground near the house, their handles vertical
exclamations at the end of a sentence
no one wants to hear. Too soon digging a hole, waiting for a widow
to declare the depth adequate
the bladed sides steep enough, smooth enough, wide enough
for the bundled root wad.
She holds the thumb-thick trunk shovel-straight, soil scooped and dragged
as ashes are spread
in two layers, starting at the convex bottom. She chants, "This is
what he wanted … what he wanted."

No one needs convincing. In this
nuclear-detonated, hydrogen-fissioned, already eight-minute-old
stale sunlight, there's not
a redwood growing within two thousand miles of these plains.
Our upturned heads see
300 feet in a thousand years. What photons aren't banged,
blocked, absorbed, diverted
by our distracted attention, pass on and on.

for Martin Stech (1947–2005)

Circus Coil

When I think of blood I think of you that night,
not because you dodged a bullet and nothing so easy
as sidestepping an office intrigue, but when you
lurched forward as if you were shot then crumpled
in that way that suggested an unexpected demise,
falling backwards from the edge of the stage, twisting deep
into that mortal coil that tightens with each passing day,
but especially this day, the audience certain
that this must be part of the performance,
and before they can blink to clear their vision,
a circus of clowns with their seltzer bottles and balloons,
horns and ping-pong-ball noses, pack into a too-small
polka-dotted car, driving out of the big tent
in a maelstrom of honking, through the odor
of elephant dung and lions' decaying breath,
and blinding belch of exhaust, the gag finished
except for you to roll down the short flight
of carpeted steps into the awed silence of nine hundred people,
more surprised than you. They did not hear
a bullet singing over their heads, or see an assassin
headed for the exit crowded with clowns.

You half-lay, half-leaned on the bottom step,
your glib ending in an ungainly perch,
there to unfold slowly the parts that gravity
harshly claimed, and you then left to reestablish an order
and what little of that can be found as you pick up
your face that the audience can see,
glasses bent like a wishbone about to break
on the wrong side of this-didn't-happen,
blood flowing too freely, anemic as that free
gas station coffee from earlier in the day,
an open spigot from the corner of your right eye,
as if your vision turned sanguine, turned back to history,

battlefields littered with parts of your warring body,
Verdun and Anzio intimate as any lover, jungle ambush
and minefield your calling, a red ribbon festooned
down your cheek, shocking the shock of your white hair
and beard into realms of a red mist, as if the front
of this stage were now heaven, the emergency room
only a quick stop along the way.

But the clowns with their lifeboat-sized shoes
didn't arrive in time to set up the scene,
their slapstick props nowhere to be seen,
and they never intended to make you the punch line,
leaving you as the day's target, sights aligned,
adjusting the scope, taking all the practice shots
needed to be dead-on deadpan, at least just enough
to break your radius, leaving you slinged and out of reach,
beyond your own grasp, halving the diameter
of your days in the ever-tightening circumference,
sure the assassin is somewhere in the audience
still deciding if you are a worthy target, still taking aim.

for David Clewell

3

VAUDEVILLE VISIGOTHS

The first couple in a cartoon bed on prime-time television was
Fred and Wilma Flintstone. All Fred could yell was, "Yabba dabba do!"
We didn't see anything more except Wilma pulling a leg bone
from her bouffant.

Their darker brethren, Ralph and Alice Kramden, in the fifties
sitcom, *The Honeymooners,* their apartment kitchen their living room,
their launching pad, when Ralph clinched a fist and spit,
BANG, ZOOM! Straight to the moon.

In our own sketches of animated desires, destitute and desperate,
we choose to jump off cliffs, slap each other against walls,
chase through one door and be chased out the other, pursuit
and escape, our bodies fields

for the game of kick-and-punch compromise. We are easy prey
for the human-sized rat traps, dynamite exploding in our mouths, falling
through loose boards in the porch, tumbling through missing
manhole covers,

the slammed door molded to our faces, and, finally, to capitulate
to the string of careening insults. We redraw our lives, erase
the purple bruises, sharpen our pencils for the next night
of comic-strip lives.

Dinner Party

The diagnosis, the reason the man's wife is not at dinner,
the operation scheduled Tuesday, tomorrow.

The husband argues the latest college sports scandal—nobody
could be that stupid, leave

that obvious a trail of payoffs. He justifies turning left at red lights.
Nobody's around, life is short.

Each cigarette subtracts three minutes—he's walked outside
four times this evening.

His math impeccable. The guests counting. His wife totaled.

HYLOZOISM

His wife on the downstairs porch swings a hammer,
backing nails out of forty-year-old
rough-cut oak just torn off an interior wall
that was once an exterior wall
before the porch became a bedroom. The oak's nails
tenacious: First the backing out
against four decades of holding tight, then turning
the board over,
picking up the flat bar, the brief one-note aria that follows,
soprano reaching stratospheric
heights as the nail flips into the air, into the bushes,
another bent note lost.

On the deck on the other side of the house, three cats locked
in the screened-in upstairs porch.
The husband watches two phoebes sweep across the lawn and perch
on a power line, then a rotten
oak branch, then on top a stake in the pea fence, then the electric meter,
always looping back
to the nest that is above his head, outside the screen, on the corner
of the house.
On each return, he hears the faint cheeping that is quickly quieted
with a mouthful
of whatever the adults have caught. If only parenting were

that easy, deciding on a safe location:
above the reach of snakes and cats, near enough to humans
to inhibit raiding jays,
gathering a few twigs and lost hair, shreds of rotting carpet,
strip of dirty-blue ribbon,
a puff of insulation, and sticking it on cedar clapboard,
then to surf the next breeze,
slipping past dozens of clawed paws—exhausted for a few weeks
until the newly feathered fledge—

then to do it again next year. The hammering continues,
as nails sing a different house.

Invasion of the Giant Tomato

Elvira, named after the late-night TV host,
      whose face is buried in eyeliner, bust
about to burst the levees of her bodice
        and flood the camera lens, hosting B-rate horror movies
that are second only to her cave-kitsch cloudy with synthetic spider
          webs and talking heads stored in boxes that dispense bad puns
for the late-night lovelorn.

Elvira always stays up late, anxious for her boyfriend's return
      from the liquor store with its barred windows and metal door
covered with booted impressions as if the superhero clientele walk up
      walls, always unwelcomed by the unsmiling cashier
behind bulletproof glass. He stops along the way to get
      a little extra before or after his purchase
of a twelve-pack of Bud or Blue Ribbon, if the deal
      went down and he feels flush.

She waits behind the door or in the ragged shadows
      of the paint-thirsty porch, cursing herself,
for letting this happen, this slide that never seems to end,
      but ends every day in something worse: utilities shut off,
kid rushed to the emergency room, hand-to-mouth
      a luxury. How could she be so stupid,
so naive, so wanton and blind in her desires.
      Ready to swing whatever she can find, the broken-

handled broom, victim of last night's jousting,
      or the dented toaster—an empty beer bottle best.
Before and after the denials, the movie in the background
      always more laughs than the horror of another night
of seething jealousy. He can leave most months blank,
      easiest by some measures,
hardest by others when he hears Elvira say
      he never wants to talk before she swings.

This afternoon clouds pour sidewalk-solid to the horizon. Rain rumors everywhere. When it's time for the cats to return to the house, there's a distant airy mewing. Too quickly the evening becomes one of vertical measures. Forty feet up a too-straight oak to the first branching fork, a young cat cries. The usual enticements for down less than ineffective.

Climbing a sixteen-feet-high ladder brings him closer but not close enough, a familiar feeling. A steady rain streaks the flashlight beam with droplets of light. Balanced on the ladder, banging an open can of turkey and giblets does no good. Wet sheets fold across the headlights driving across the county to borrow a taller ladder. Midnight, the rungs hoisted, rain falls deep into itself. He can't see below into the black backwater that is air. Branches swim in and out of the flashlight. He shouts upward. The cat's cries don't stop. He gives up and goes to bed.

Before leaving for work, he's back at it. People-of-the-first-light who worshipped the first thing they saw, the Wampounog, nowhere now to be found, but person-of-the-first-ladder-in-first-light, he climbs through fog searching for the sun and instead finds a cat too afraid to claw itself down to be rescued. Safe as an Easter penitent, his arms nail him to the trunk, the cat still high in the tree . He leaves for work, windshield wipers beating a frantic fourteen-mile measure.

Mid-afternoon, he extends the ladder another four feet, screws an eight-feet long two-inch board to the outside of a thirty-five-gallon red plastic garbage can. A bowl of jack mackerel sits inside as he slides the can up the ladder, then beyond the top rung until it's near the feet of the rain-drenched cat. Without hesitation it dives in, then cautiously he slides the cat, the mackerel, the bowl, the can, slowly down and marches with the cat above his head, a Roman Legion standard entering triumphantly into Alexandria after the burning of the harbor fleet, before the firing of the world's greatest library, though it's beginning to feel more like an Egyptian cat cult and the house a pyramid with a screened-in porch.

Seeds of Revolution

All that's needed are three or four feet of plastic pipe,
one end capped closed, the other end left

a speechless open "O." A small hole drilled in front of the cap,
an aerosol can of starter ether left over

from winter engine troubles, a butane lighter set for high flame,
and perhaps a palisade of cottonwoods

along a steep bank, and a few beers, or more than a few beers,
and then it's time to defend the river

from behemoth barges that traffic slowly past. From the grocery
bag a right-diameter potato,

forced tight into the open end of the pipe, the hole primed
with ether and ignited. The potato goes ballistic

for three or four hundred feet, ringing the steel hull, then falling
into the murky current—victory for the bottom-feeders.

Gorilla God

The interview room cold, the angles softly hardened against sound.
The inevitable question arises:
What makes a good poem? I'm never prepared.
On radios across the country,
silence pulls a Saturday night special. The microphone points
in every direction I turn.

I take a deep breath, submerge a third time into resignation,
then ask forgiveness
for an answer I haven't yet given. I could be glib and ask
what doesn't make a good poem,
and not be glib at all but mean it, or resort to cliché: It's not
the wave or the surfboard
but the surfer who sculpts the ride. Too quickly I'm a sun-bleached
beach bum
describing the ball tossed within a circle of people kicking imaginary sand
on a stage in front of a packed auditorium. The crowd's murmur the rush
of high tide as floodlights swamp the stage. The audience is asked to count
the times the ball is thrown like the abacus of waves rattling along
the shore, watchers sure
to be lost within the churning susurration, the wind
salting their eyes
as a loose line of pelicans wing-pumps past.

If the audience wants to complicate the task, prove their prowess,
how far out they can stretch
their attention, swim beyond lifeguards and safety buoys,
they can sum the catches
within the circle of throwers. When asked for totals,
there's disagreement, a few people
crying like gulls over a washed-up dead seal. When asked
if anyone noticed anything else,
there are a few tentative hands raised who perhaps recall
Lowell's definition of poetry,

a controlled hallucination, though maybe they'd drunk one
too many complimentary
glasses of wine. They confess to seeing a person dressed in a cheap
gorilla suit run
through the middle of the circle while the ball was tossed
back and forth.

Truth trembles, variations of misperception and blindness,
what we can't see
a matter of visions and revisions. Is that what Blake meant, imagination
is not a state but the essence
of human existence? And so I answer the question, a good poem
is one that is looking
for the gorilla running across the shores of our lives.

Pinko

I have no idea where the seats are located. Maybe her
boyfriend said row five near the stage.
Between acts, stagehands switch drum sets, stack amps,

run electric cords, adjust lighting, as I sink toward them,
fishlike, finning in the bowl of the auditorium.
I don't recognize anyone, turn to walk back from the stage

when she comes running and points to the far left
of the first raised row of seats.
Under her chair, a stack of papers she's grading

before the show, between acts. The gears of the academy
grind on. The lights dim, the crowd
jumps to its feet. A roar rises as a spotlight burns

a white hole around the vacant center-stage microphone.
Sheryl Crow appears out
of the murky depths. The light catches the crowd's anemone-arms.

They feed on every note, every chord, every syllable of lyrics.
They can't stop waving and rocking
in a sea of sound. I can't make it past her wardrobe:

pink pants with off-shade-of-pink knee patches,
pink stiletto-heeled boots,
dark pink blouse with large ruffled pink collar,

and solid-body pink guitar. I think this is
what my daughter wore
when she was nine, excluding the spike-heeled boots,

and maybe that's why my wife won't let me play
my one Sheryl Crow CD.
She hears the pink inflections.

I shout this over the over-amplified
music to the woman who fished me out
of the crowd, and in the overstimulation

of the moment, she's stunned, as if I've said something
sacrilegious. Through two
more songs, she hardly moves, staring as Sheryl beats

her guitar, prances on the pink concert piano,
struts through the smoke and light.
She turns to me, speaks in a tone of cracked aquarium

glass, pink water pouring out, pink fish flopping
on the floor. That's not what I meant.
No, I say I'm a die-hard fan, pink one of my favorite colors.

I have a pink dress shirt that I wear when I'm on the road making
sales calls. I shut up. It's too late.
The next songs will never ease this pink disquiet.

It's like saying, but I have a Jewish friend.
I have a black friend,
I have a pink shirt hanging in my closet.

for Robin and Karen

UTTERLY AGAIN

A man calls from across the country.
        He's urgent as cumulus clouds
crowded in a phone booth at Atlantic
        and Boardwalk. I hear him clearly
speaking out of the grip of my hand,
        the rain of his syllables flooding my ear.
He's calling me about the last two lines
        to a poem published twenty years ago
in a small South Dakota literary magazine.
        I don't hear thunder or the drumming
of a downpour, but he's persistent, urgent—
        forty years old, working at an engineering

firm that won't promote him until
        he completes a degree in anything.
The poem describes cattle mutilation,
        the details that turn our heads away
even as our eyes move farther down
        the page. There's the irony of someone,

them, traveling light years, hundreds
        of millions of miles, to surgically remove
the right ear and eye, the tongue and udder,
        all the blood and the sexual organs,
from a grazing angus, the highest life form
        in a tick-infested back forty.

We talk for half an hour. He says each
        morning for a week he's repeated
those last two lines: *and the one they take*
        is a stranger to us all. I mumble something
about Descartes, consciousness, the mind—
        body duality of Western culture. I don't

believe I've helped. He says, it's just what he needed
    to finish his paper.
I ask who is teaching the class and at what college,
    but he says he was asked not to reveal names.
Later, after his generous thanks and promise
    to have a check in the mail for copies

of all my dusty books (the check never arrives),
    I begin to wonder, to have doubts, who it was
I spoke to, and maybe I shouldn't have given
    my address to a stranger. Isn't this what we warn
children not to do? How could anyone have
    found that obscure issue of an obscure magazine,

to have read a short esoteric poem and then assigned
    it for class discussion? Who was I really
talking to? Maybe they think I know something,
    that these words are a code and a plot?
In the room by the phone it's growing dark. The ceiling
    begins to rain. Take me to your leader.

Day's Receipt

What a block of life has past.
    —Robert Lowell

The book marked by a yellowed cashier's receipt dated
December 21, 1991, the shortest day of that year,

and twenty-three years later it's still the shortest day, and grows shorter yet,
though the day remains

twenty-four hours long and not at all. But I'm worried about last week,
having not fully stopped at a traffic light, rolling through

and turning right as a mounted camera clicked away. This doesn't deny
the last megafauna extinction, giant ground sloths

and mastodons. Arctic ice cores reveal dust laid down
by another meteor collision

maybe twelve thousand years before traffic cameras. There's no turning back
from a moving violation and living

through the failure to stop anything—hurtling planet, meteor,
ticket and fine.

Maybe it was never clear, decades ago a new job, now years
of alarm clocks ring in my head,

the miles between here and there tallied under a diminishing sun.
What was I doing? In the remembering,

a day passed without beginning or end. A night where surely
the stars with their vast vestments

of space collapsed inward, and if I stared up at all,
I was lost, eyes opened or closed.

At least the receipt has a time and place printed but fading:
at 10:24 a.m., money exchanged,

the transaction completed. I would like to think I was satisfied
as I turned to leave, having found what I wanted

or a satisfactory substitute. But there must have been more.
A name for the young clerk, say Hannah,

and in her haste to beat back the clock, she dropped two pennies
that spun off across the floor, twin copper galaxies,

and were lost under the next counter. She apologized to the person
behind me for her clumsiness,

for taking too long, which wasn't long at all, if she recalled
saber-toothed tigers and mammoths,

and it was even shorter than a meteor burning through
the stratosphere. The receipt for one day

out of 21,000 comes back to me as fiction like all the rest.

ARGUMENTS OF WEATHER

At the maw of the Dumpster, beyond the double glass doors,
                         across the striped asphalt lot,
past one sapling planted between concrete parking bumpers,
                         beside the next building
zigzagged with gang graffiti, the world is trying
                         to erase itself one flake and shadow

at a time. *No, it's not,* a friend would say,
                         and maybe I would too, then
hesitate. He'd want to know what *try* means? How can a planet
                         wobbling on its axis try? Or a cloud?
Or snow? Where's the will to try anything, the ambition

to accomplish this trying? The forecast is six to nine inches.
                         What can be said of snow is that it is
a four-letter word. More so as you get older. But then there are
                         other four-letter words:
this and *that*, *slip* and *fall*, but not *try* or *erase*. *Bury*, yes:

It requires no attention. An avalanche doesn't attend to what it
                         buries any more than the forecast blizzard.
To erase without intention is inattention or a mistake.
                         To make a mistake
is to have intended something else.

The broken lawn mower tangled in the dry stalks
                         of wintered weeds
in the front yard, buried under snow, not erased but imagined
                         into the longed-for ski lift,
that is an unaffordable mistake—the this and that of poverty,
                         and uneraseable. The lawn mower

pushed off into another dimension, a mad man mowing frozen
                              fields, shortchanged into failure,
the future gospel melting into revival, a 6.75-horsepower Briggs
                              & Stratton resurrection:
choke set, gas primed, rope yanked, the engine clatters to life,
                              but my friend interrupts again:

life nothing but movement: the mechanics of contained
                              combustion, pistons and drive shaft,
greased and oiled to prevent this life from wearing down
                              too quickly, just enough to make it
to the day-after-the-warranty breakdown.

Our own guaranties are never so clear. Across the lot, an inch of slush
                              glazes half-crushed paper cups,
torn pages from a magazine. The radio slant has changed,
                              Locke's tabula rasa
won't clean up this day or night.

The Day After Us

Shadows drop into drought. I kick up a darker dust bucketing
water to the garden
where peppers flicker, flame. Grass bleaches back to its roots.
Seared leaves turn to a paper-thin translucence.
I don't know what to say any longer yet I say it. Thirty years has left
a meager accounting. We were squeezed
into a small house on a busy street. The war went on without us.
The FBI kept our diaries.

We sat in a room late nights with one table surrounded by walls
of an ancient necropolis.
Thick stone faces stared down centuries, missing here and there
an eyebrow, a nose, a wind-worn eye.
Headless statues lined a wide avenue of sand, leading through tumbled
columns under a vast blue ache of sky.
It was the old dance and we took a few awkward steps
of no accomplishment,
but it was our dance. Once a week, your ex-wife flamed
at the front door,
unannounced, lost in her own angry desert, refusing "No," knowing
that you were home,
and, "No," there wasn't another woman hiding under the bed, though once
there was. She rushed past
to search for what was and wasn't there, accusing me, a fastidious liar,
of authoring the plot. One time she found you,
in the claw-legged bathtub, where often you set sail, hours spent reading.
She always left in ashes.

One evening, I woke remembering nothing of the previous night's intrigues,
except I had died.
I know, my eyes sealed, the lenses of my glasses smeared
with candle wax.
The rest of the journey waited until now. At seven in the evening,
a call from the hospital,

I hear the nurse command you to stay in bed. I'm told to call back
in ten minutes.
After so many years, I recognize your faltering greeting.
A man who once stood on the bridge
of the flagship leading the Cuban missile blockade, and a month ago
plotted to write a science fiction novel,
now a simple sailor bobbing out into a morphine sea.

for Lt. Commander Luther Skelton

FAMILY OF STARS

The sky no longer just sky
but the buffeted debris of wind and light,

black holes
and galaxies in collision. We are ready to improvise ragged visions

on the bottomless up
we stare into, the endless tales tongued by clouds, half-seen,

not seen—half-men, half-gods—
much less heard, quickly scudding toward a weathered dissolution,

an evaporation, an annihilation,
a preparation for yet another resurrection beyond megaliths

and memory.
No book-thumbed page of the fossil record, no number one

on the phylum charts,
no top-forty crustacean to spin over growing static and worse

reception as the distance swells,
no lance for the lonely boil. No audience for the doo-wop

of humming planets, the rock of celestial music,
the unbearable siren song of emptiness, a tree falls in the forest

rearranging only the decomposition.
There's no doubt that I remember you, father, and your father laid

out in a Cincinnati hospital bed,
dentures spilling half out of his mouth, an enamel deck of cards,

the last ace played and lost,
and your mother unable to remember anyone except perhaps

this pocket of earth that's always difficult
to find: the row, the plot, a whole city of grass avenues to stroll

and any stone might do,
but I kept searching as your sister's eyes bulged, froglike above

the pond of sheets,
displacing pressure of tumors, a permanent hysterical stare

as the sky crashed silently
through the room. No, not permanent. I remember you

in the back yard, snapping me
into your baseball dream, throw fast, throw straight,

throw at the mitt. We are
each other's speedball eternities. I remember as I remember

until there is no remembering
and the clouds blow into a wider quiet of stars.

MEMORIAL DAY

A man on the radio, and I can't help but for the briefest moment hum
a few bars of the Stones' "Satisfaction,"

tells me more and more
about some useless information
that defies my imagination,
I can't get no ...

and there is no satisfaction found in knowing, but not knowing enough
to act. There's just the driving through,

listening to a news report on Hell House, a Texas Pentecostal
church project, raising money to harvest souls.

Six months after the shootings, they reenact Columbine.
They reenact a boy dying of AIDS,

a girl gang-raped, an abortion, an addled drug addict.
In the passenger seat, my elderly mother says

that's like her friend's son, his uniforms, machine guns,
vintage military jeeps and trucks, an authentic

down-to-thread-and-buttons reenactor of battles, a host
of hundreds, perhaps thousands, shooting blanks.

What reenacting soul approaches Olathe, Lenexa, Shawnee, Lansing?
We arrive at the rolling river hills

of the Leavenworth National Military Cemetery. Multitudes
of postcard-sized flags jitter with wind.

Century oaks command the ridges. Stopped in one small valley
at one anonymous curve,

my mother can't remember if it's twelve or seventeen rows
up from here or over there.

We begin the hobbled charge up the slope, the sun to our backs,
our shadows stretching before us

making strange leaps that defy our lack of progress. To the right,
to the left, the endless forgetting.

Follow the dates on the stones back to November 9, 1984.
Did this father ever follow the dates back,

hoping to find some refuge from the carbine strapped to his back,
toes numb enough to forget pain,

sitting on frozen bodies above the vast erasure, snow stuck
to his mud-caked field jacket, those falling

white epaulets raising his rank by the hour, drift of icy star upon star,
remembering back to some warm day

on Virginia Avenue in a smoke-choked city, anywhere away from the
regiment of snowmen,

facing their empty stares, and the half-healed wounded sent back
to the front, the shell-shocked

living on Blue 88s, anything to keep them fit to kill or be killed,
never learning replacements

of replacements' names, too exhausting to forget so much—
bodies left nameless.

What did my father remember in order to forget? What does
my mother forget in order to remember?

We pull a few weeds. We shove plastic grape hyacinths and tulips
into the dirt around the flat stone.

Fewer of These...

Hiroshima, August 6, 2010

That's what the headline reads.
Already someone is manufacturing fireflies, lightning bugs,

a wingless battery-powered luminescence,
a stand in for what once was, to remind us, to deceive us

into believing in fields
of quivering light, a greenish flickering, an ephemeral lace,

and not Twain's
thunderbolt, just one more faux bug.

On summer evenings,
years ago, in a sycamore-crowned creek

under a full moon,
where friends gathered monthly, where already many

will not return,
surely the fireflies, pulled up and out of tall grasses

by the full moon's
double-barreled magnetism, would come to outline these nights

again, but even these small creatures
much like the candles set afloat on paper boats, drifting across dusk,

ghost lights of ashen cities,
the upwelling of souls before they upturn and fizzle in the current—

how foolish to believe that a stream
of flickering lights outlining night's far reaches might remember us

long after we remember them.

After another night blinded by impulse,
the brisk shock of living on the living,
October 4, 1582, when Hans and Gretchen,
prepare for bed,
sunset and the smell of smoky
fat from blown-out candles choke
their hut, then waking,
the sun much too bright,
their abundant hope harvested
and growing shorter with the season.

Evening at thick wooden tables and quarter-sawn
benches where they lean on calloused elbows,
their dirt-lined faces little different
from the surrounding fields, their hands
slapping down beside wooden cups,
defiant approval to another dying year,
their struggle for closure and continuance,
then to wake the next day, October 15, 1582,
but not after an eleven-day hangover
or fungus-infested, ergot-grain induced hallucination,

not having succumbed to a succubus
or incubus, witches already in ashes,
not an accidental entering of Parnassus,
realm of Niflheim, or joined by the Nibelung,
but by the fiat of Pope Gregory, plotting
to realign the fallen human race with the stars.
The revolutions of rich, poor, and planets,
an astrological reordering, though nothing changed

for Hans and Gretchen, who didn't notice
they'd aged eleven days in one night,
their room lit only by fire,
their century unknown to them,

left only with the ache in their joints, the winter
still ahead, spring a prayer.

Paint by Numbers

... stairs for the void running down to the garden
—Wisława Szymborska

From fallen fence to ragged tree line, on late
September afternoons,

each stiff knee-high stalk of bleached grass
vibrates a glassy light.

Bare feet trample narrow paths that lead down
from rolling hills

through wooded hollows, across pastures, ending
at the first worn step

polished by untold soles. Grasshoppers clatter in low
careening flights,

colliding with bare legs, fluttering down naked spines
in this procession of sunburnt backs.

Near a muddy, cattail-choked pond in the middle of a fallow
field, the spiral staircase ascends.

No one more than shivers as grasshoppers scrape across
their skin, spitting brown saliva.

No one in this unending line ever looks back until they stop
and place their right foot on the first step.

Even the brittle locusts and their mechanical chirring are not
distraction enough to slow the slow progress.

Little relief to hear the vast silence beyond the arbored insect choir
they've passed through,

or that the line extends into the next county, country, century.
There are men wearing three-cornered hats,

codpieces, holey jeans; women in hoop skirts, wasp-thin girdles,
Spandex. Most already surrendered

their fashion to stand naked. The first tread sags from the weight
of so many journeys, but no one cares,

leaving their itineraries in the grass for beetles and moles,
turning lighter than air as they step higher.

The spiral column carved with suffering, the stair risers
ornate with beaks and snouts,

with fins and claws, with teeth and feathers. Souls grimace
with the hollow pupils

of wide-eyed shock. The naked line an odd contour,
a heartless bloodless vein

in the paint-by-numbers eternal autumnal landscape. Those who reach
the breathless top

have no time for speeches. They plunge after the final step,
carried by a breeze across the garden.

THE MISSOURI AUTHORS SERIES

2014: *The Empire Rolls* by Trudy Lewis
2015: *The Teeth of the Souls* by Steve Yates
2016: *Swimming on Hwy N* by Mary Troy
2017: *Too Quick for the Living* by Walter Bargen